The Big Radish

Written by Jan Burchett and
Sara Vogler

Illustrated by Grace Sandford

Collins

Viv has a radish.

It is big!

Viv tugs the radish.

4

Jim tugs Viv.

Liz tugs Jim.

Buzz tugs Liz.

Duck tugs Buzz.

They tug and tug.

Chick tugs and tugs Duck.

The radish pops up.

Yum! Yum!

15

After reading

Letters and Sounds: Phase 3

Word count: 40

Focus phonemes: /j/ /v/ /y/ /z/ /qu/ /ch/ /sh/ zz

Common exception words: the, they

Curriculum links: Mathematics: children use everyday language to talk about size

Early learning goals: Reading: use phonic knowledge to decode regular words and read them aloud accurately, read some common irregular words

Developing fluency

- Your child may enjoy hearing you read the book.
- You could take turns to read a page with lots of expression.

Phonic practice

- Practise reading words that contain new phonemes (letter sounds).
- Say the sounds in the words below.

  qu/a/ck   ch/i/ck   r/a/d/i/sh   b/u/zz

- Ask your child to repeat the sounds and then say the word.
- Look at the "I spy sounds" pages (14–15) together. How many items can your child spot that contain the /ch/ sound or the /j/ sound? (*cherries, chocolate, cheese, chick, chair, jumper, jam, jar, jelly, jug*)

Extending vocabulary

- Read pages 4 to 5 to your child. Can they suggest some other words to describe what is happening in the story? (e.g. *Viv pulls the radish, Jim grabs Viv*)
- Now do the same thing with pages 12 to 13. (e.g. *the radish lifts out of the ground and flies into the air*)